Woodland of Wonders

Echoes in the Night
A Brown Bat's Adventure

Kenzie Field

In the woodland of wonders

a dark hole exists,

where a brown bat is born

in the caves by the cliffs.

She's dependent on mom.
She is furless and blind.
This small pup clings to fur
on her mother's behind.

In the nursery roost,
drinking milk mom provides,
she becomes big and strong
like the pups by her side.

The patagium skin
of her brown wings have grown.
She begins practice flaps
to soon fly on her own.

When she's ready to fly
she becomes very brave.
Leaving mom is one step,
and the next is the cave.

With a swoop here and there,
she feels free in the sky.
But her stomach needs food.
She'll give hunting a try.

Though her eyesight is good
she will hunt in the dark,
using sensitive ears
that will target her mark.

Using echolocation,
reflection of sound,
she identifies prey
and all obstacles round.

In pitch darkness her call
has discovered a fly.
She moves faster with speed
she'll dive fast and swoop by.

She has caught a quick fly
with her stretched membrane wing,
and she tosses it hard
in her mouth with a fling.

What a tasty small treat!
It is time to find more.
At least one thousand bugs,
half her weight, that's for sure!

She hunts high and hunts low
in the long summer days.
We'll move forward a year
to learn more of her ways.

Her experience grows,
as a year passes by.
She's mature and has skills.
She's a forest ally.

She can pollinate plants

and control insect pests

and help fertilize soil

with her scat, it's the best!

Yet, summer days now fade,
and the cold breeze blows in.
This is signaling change,
and soon fall will begin.

Through the bright orange leaves,
red and yellow ones too,
fall has turned the green forest
a warm coloured hue.

She takes off in the sky
as the sun nearly sets,
to the watering hole
as the fall day resets.

She can hear different calls,
coming loud from ahead.
They're attracting her, so
she will change course instead.

She discovers a male,

with his wings on display.

His fast flapping appeals,

and she can't look away.

Her small eyes are now locked

on the bat's funny strut.

She consents his approach,

she feels love in her gut.

The fall days turn to frost.

Winter cold is quite near.

Hibernation time comes

for the rest of the year.

With more expecting moms,
she wakes from her sleep.
In a nursery roost,
they keep warm in a heap.

A full circle has come,

where the dark hole exists.

A new brown bat is born

in the caves by the cliffs.

Dedicated to

my son Beau & new baby to come

Inspired by my environmental science background,

and educating our little humans about our natural environment.

FIELD KITS Publishing

July 2024

Author

Kenzie Field

Editor

Kathryn Boucher & Jaimee Guenther

Illustrator

Canva AI

ISBN: 978-1-7383200-9-7

© All rights reserved. No part of this book may be reproduced in any form or by any electronic or mechanical means, including information storage and retrieval systems, without permission in writing from the publisher and copyright holder, except in the case of brief quotations embodied in critical articles and reviews. This is a work of creative nonfiction. Some parts have been fictionalized to varying degrees.

Woodland of Wonders Book Series

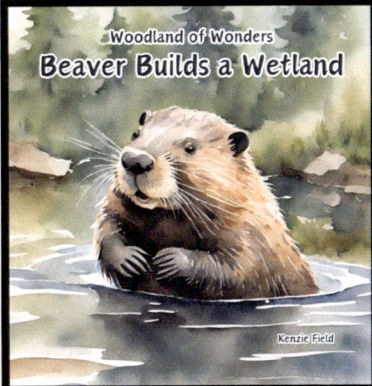

www.ingramcontent.com/pod-product-compliance
Lightning Source LLC
Chambersburg PA
CBRC091724070526
44585CB00009B/171